AF390943

Jamia Masjid mosque (completed 1402), Srinagar, Jammu and Kashmir, India

EASTERN STRUCTURES

editor

R. W. Watkins

creative consultants

Jim Wilson
Jacqueline Jones

printing / production

Nocturnal Iris
World Headquarters
in conjunction with KDP
and Amazon.com

Cover, page 2 and above:
Kashmir and Me (YouTube)

Eastern Structures is published
four times per year by
Nocturnal Iris Publications

PO Box 111
Moreton's Harbour, NL
A0G 3H0 Canada

Postal submissions of poems, essays,
reviews or related material should be
accompanied by an SASE (in
Canada) or an SAE + IRC (outside of
Canada). Electronic submissions
should be e-mailed to
nocturnaliris@gmail.com.

EASTERN STRUCTURES

Number 16 • Autumn, 2020 • ISBN: 9798595465724

CONTENTS

Forward

I find it ever so ironic that the North American poets working in Eastern poetic forms who receive the most attention from the media tend to be those who are also the most compromised and least accomplished in their craft. I know I've touched on this subject in the past, but my interest has been rekindled in recent months, after I received a rather conspicuous submission of 'ghazals' from an Iranian-American professor-turned-poet.

It appears that the fellow in question is the author of four books of poetry, has published in several key journals, and has been the recipient of a number of awards and prizes. He is a professor of Creative Writing and Literature at Queen's College in New York. He has also been written up in an article by *Frontline* at PBS.org, and comes complete with a Wikipedia entry. Given such a glowing résumé, it's a shame the poor professor can't write a proper ghazal to save his hide. Seriously; someone should send the man a rhyming dictionary for his next birthday.

I blame such hollow public figures on a culture that, on the one hand, accepts the views and creative output of academics—particularly those with PhDs who hold professorships—as infallible and exemplary, and, on the other, avoids the work and opinions of those who do not possess the 'proper' ethnic ties to their area of expertise, for fear of endorsing 'cultural (mis)appropriation'. The fact of the matter is that this is a conundrum that does nothing for society in the long run except produce emperors severely lacking in garments.

As far as the literary world is concerned, the blame ultimately rests with inadequate editors and publishers, of course. In the case of the ghazal in an American context, any news or literary editor worth his or her salt could have easily found a composer of genuine English-language ghazals if he or she had made the effort. If such editors had insisted on ties to the academy, then they could have called on the likes of Eric Torgersen or John Philip Drury. If they had further insisted on ethnic ties to the Islamic or Asian world, then they could have focussed on the work of the late Kashmiri-American professor, Agha Shahid Ali.

As far as the ghazal is concerned, the American experience is by no means a far cry from the Canadian one. It appears that Canadian editors and publishers have devoted so much paper to publishing and promoting the likes of John Thompson, Phyllis Webb, Rob Winger, Lorna Crozier and Sheniz Janmohamed that they now have no desire to publish or even investigate genuine English-language examples of the form for fear of discrediting the output of their 'stables of talent' and making themselves look ignorant and incompetent in the process. Imagine Reverend Lovejoy from *The Simpsons* holding his hands over his ears and singing 'Bringing in the Sheaves' while people inform him of his young daughter's sociopathic ways.

As one can well imagine, I rejected the 'acclaimed' professor's five half-arsed attempts at the Persian ghazal with little in the way of hesitation. Never one to completely discourage or discredit potential contributors, however, I worded the rejection 'slip' in such a manner to make sure that he went away happy:

> I'm sorry, but you sound much
> too important for a magazine
> like *Eastern Structures*. Please
> say hello to Dr Kissinger for us.

I signed the email message "Sincerely", and stated my professorial credential and my many accolades in parentheses after my name. I can only hope that he took me as seriously as a professor and award-winning poet as what I took him as a writer of ghazals.

Look for the next issue of *Eastern Structures* in March. There's no guarantee that you'll find it, mind you, but look for it.

R. W. Watkins

(Professor of Fuck-All-ogy,
winner and recipient of Nothing)

A Ghazal and a Birdsong

S. Haina

A soft morning tiptoes in bringing a brand-new birdsong
It's absurd; I've never heard such an impromptu birdsong

I can't help but eavesdrop; magnetic melody pulls me
My heart's laid bare; I hope this is not a taboo birdsong

Though your music should lull me to a land of cushioned hills
I'd voluntarily lose more and more sleep to birdsong

Every note just as sweet as a pomegranate seed
Wish I could see the epiphany you bring through birdsong

Like a letter full of love scented softly with jasmine
Wish I could translate my velvet daydream into birdsong

Eager mornings confirm that they bring with them a plus-one
I jump straight out of bed to tune in right on cue: birdsong

I try follow your call but get lost in a maze of trees
Wish I can one day find a sure way to thank you, birdsong

I am starting to note more intervals between your notes
Wish you won't fade and leave me like autumn leaves, blue birdsong

Though your tone carries the luxuries of your forefathers
I will never hear a more humble, pure and true birdsong.

Never Wronged Before

William Dennis

Pipped blanket-dark to brilliant chill, though never wronged before;
in blossom breath surrounding words not gone among before.

Old madness among flowers, apricot and orange, both;
my buzzing fills whole orchards, though they've heard this song before.

Be left or reft, you pick your pumpkin in the seed, and water.
A choice hurts less than choosing does. I have picked wrong before.

The shaggy, shedding, broad-beamed sun fills every furrow plowed;
we leaf and twine on what seemed barren earth not long before.

Glad-hand zucchini, tempt to apples, the press to give grows urgent;
fill every hand and pocket you let pass along before.

Through seasons of the ripening sun, I grow to call *"me"* *"we"*,
ripe, plump-souled sages dropped, whose *"us"* was all Hong Kong before.

Grandchildren, ripening gold, grant them any kindness.
The afterlife is lived in them that have gone long before.

Ghazal

Aafaq Hameed

There my city glows like a bride, and here I break myself.
Then only when you seem to arrive I remake myself.

I have a chinar in my garden. And a shattered heart.
Tell me, when is this autumn? Do I have to rake myself?

Do you disown your people when their presence means nothing?
I should forsake them, eh? Or shall I just forsake myself?

"How about we go somewhere together? Badamwari in bloom?"
Until I realize, who're *we*?! So, I just take myself

It was not just Ghalib with his face all smeared with dirt
For ugly blots on glass, I too often mistake myself

Listen

John W. Steele

Listen to the river-rock percussion tones. Who hears
the water-dervish swirling over stones? Who hears?

Tibetan prayer flags slap a fence pole,
soprano through the malleus bones. Who hears?

Kids on skateboards grind across a bridge.
A mallard quacks to her young clones—Who hears?

A van with studded snow-tires thunders past,
pounding rap through residential zones. Who hears?

When Rumi cries out, *Shams*—angels faint.
The far-flung void intones, *Who hears*?

The one who turns when someone calls out, *John*—
feels the question stirring in his bones, *Who hears?*

Prophets

Mace Hosseini

Where are the prophets now, when we need them the most? Where are they, Lord?
Where are the father, the son, and the Holy Ghost? Where are they, Lord?

Who is speaking for the crowd? Who is protesting on our behalf?
Who is fighting the bad guys? Who is our foremost? Where are they, Lord?

Where is a Christ, entering the temple of the money exchange
To challenge charging the interest and impost? Where are they, Lord?

Jesus left a herd just to rescue one lost sheep – a good shepherd.
Where are the shepherds—the sheep and the goats are roast—Where are they, Lord?

Where are the guardian angels, watching over the innocents?
Where are they now, and when are they going to boast? Where are they, Lord?

Where are the saints, the bishops and the nuns to lend a helping hand?
    Where are the open churches? The guests need a host. Where are they, Lord?

Where are the Good Samaritans, and where have all the heroes gone?
    A tsunami is coming: Who is guarding the coast? Where are they, Lord?

Oh Lord, whatever happened to the sense of the goodness in souls?
    Who attends the Sunday mass, right after the toast? Where are they, Lord?

Woodcut illustration from Francesco Maria Guazzo's
Compendium Maleficarum (Milan, 1626)

Above and Below

Laura Z. Fairgrieve

A laughing jackal portends a witch in the loft of those who've sassed her,
some Nigerians say; nothing is conjured without a caster.

The church of our fears has walls too thick for windows,
and what other blindness could cause terror to sprint faster?

Those who live below rattle foundations when night is deepest;
when dreams have wandered away and the ceiling snows down plaster.

The quilt of stars shakes above as the cold falls asleep.
Who do the mosquitoes sing to, while they bathe in blood and disaster?

Throw down Morningstar, seize his Laurels, spark and melt them after.
Boil, boil, toil and remember—his questions were made by his master.

Home to Roost

Alison Stone

I'm energized by animals, kale, song.
Our new cat named for a Nine Inch Nails song.

So much heart-breaking music. Garland's drug-
fueled rainbow, Billie's blues, Joplin's wail-song.

Bay of hounds chained in dusty yards. War chant.
Lament of the cancer-stricken. Jail song.

How to give the spirit voice? When fasting's
not enough, try sex. When words fail, song.

Bathtub-born, Sasha slipped from his mother
into water. In the background, whale song.

Jacob fooled his father. Karma wrote his
son an impostor-beneath-the-veil song.

History's chickens home to roost. Poe knew –
we're all exposed by the heart's telltale song.

In my dream, I drift from field to forest,
hear, through silver branches, wind's pale song.

Wrens have my mother's eyes. Her last concert,
Whitney missed the high notes. Shaky, frail song.

Notes refusing to soar. Is this what killed
her, this broken promise, betrayal song?

Bombs, smog, greed, guns, oil-coated seagulls.
Melting ice. We're all bored with that stale song.

How hard it is to love the world. Find and
inhale beauty, Alison. Exhale song.

Pandemic Birthday Ghazal

Mike Alexander

Lo! the customary FB bustle for my birthday.
R. W. demands a ghazal for my birthday.

I try to make the jigsaw notches fit together.
In quarantine, I do a puzzle for my birthday.

The president keeps tweeting like a drunk macaw.
Could someone fit him for a muzzle for my birthday?

Nine months alone together – a testament to Love.
My wife gives my scruffy neck a nuzzle for my birthday.

& while I have no fixed religious affiliation,
I send my Facebook friends a Mazel for my birthday.

Please

Mace Hosseini

Do not repeat the narratives, don't try to please; tell it like it is.
    Write a brand new release: don't transcribe, don't appease – tell it like it is.

Paint about the garden of earthly delights, talk about the darned greed.
    Shoot flowers and weeds, not just the birds and the bees; tell it like it is.

Give us the truth in the news, not the news and the well-established views.
    Don't talk about heat when we are in a deep freeze; tell it like it is.

Don't go describing the water when we are drowning in the great flood.
    Don't discuss freedom when the chains are here to seize; tell it like it is.

Don't divide and conquer, don't be a part of the war that you oppose.
    Recite about your errors, and pray on your knees; tell it like it is.

Write a book about the other side, publish a new unholy book.
    You know all the commandments; this should be a breeze. Tell it like it is.

Create a new sculpture that doesn't fit the scenery, that stands out.
    Chisel a hard stone into a new piece at ease. Tell it like it is.

We all die once – a piece of cake; what awaits us after, no one knows.
    Heaven or hell? How we live life gives us the keys – tell it like it is.

Ghazal

Aafaq Hameed

What morn will cease this night? Tell me!
What hand will veil the plight? Tell me!

Darkened are the brightest of towns
What lamp will bequeath light? Tell me!

Not seeking the cure of death but
What touch will heal the blight? Tell me!

The fall froze, seeing all the snow
What spell will break this height? Tell me!

Wild winds have devoured my city
Do storms pity a kite? Tell me!

All the poets are dead, all gone
Who will now dare to write? Tell me!

Three Sijo

Michael Wilson

The Gospel of Country Music

It takes a bottle of Jesus   to kill the devil in me
That's what George Jones whispers in   Johnny Cash's Folsom Prison ear
Johnny strums G, C and D   granting broken hearts parole

New Year's Eve, 2020

bad dreams are in production   that's the astral word on the street
no trailers, no previews,   just the scraping sound of footsteps
stagehands moving scenery   behind our collective frozen screen

Hungry Ghosts

what we want matters too much   to dismiss with sentences of death
scribed by temporary ruler   of eye, ear, nose, tongue, touch
rotting in forgotten grave: after body's gone, we live on

Patiently waiting for the apocalypse to finally come
And paying no mind to the optimistic cynics and doubters,
You stand on your soapbox preaching that the times are now biblical.

— Rose Menyon Heflin

Tanka

Rose Menyon Heflin

Such glittering scales
Rainbow trout's colorful back
Barely visible
Under clear flowing waters
Coursing waywardly in spring

Sandhill crane pauses
Beside a tributary
To eat a small vole
The lump in its slender throat
Moving slowly to the base

Along the bayou
Under a bright Cajun moon
Trills a cricket's song
Fireflies dance in the dark night
Spanish moss sways in the trees

The thunder rumbles
Through the deep, dark, midnight sky
Portending lightning
Growling angry at the stars
Warning of nature's fury

A murder of crows
Turning pages one by one
Dancing out the rain
Choosing only the best straws
Before flying off, away

Autumnal music
Leaves skittering down the fence
Crunching underfoot
Honk of southward migrations
Snap of pumpkins on the vine

Shivering seedheads
Senescence overcomes fall,
So swift and cooling;
Prepares the world for winter,
Bitter cold and uncaring

Form and Spirit in English-Language Haiku

Jim Wilson

David Cobb, 2005

"The argument about what makes a haiku has shifted largely from form to spirit. But there is still much discussion about what that 'spirit' is."

– David Cobb, 'English Haiku: A Composite View'

Earlier this month (November 6th, 2020), David Cobb died. In the announcement, the British Haiku Society linked to an article by Cobb, which I quote from above. The article, 'English Haiku: A Composite View', is a good overview of the various perspectives currently used among English-language Haiku poets. (As an aside, I think that when Cobb says 'English Haiku', he primarily means Great Britain.)

Cobb outlines various ways that contemporary English-language haiku poets understand English-language haiku (ELH) and how that influences their way of writing and what they strive to accomplish when writing it. I was particularly struck by Cobb's observation that discussions about what ELH *is* have shifted focus from form to spirit (Cobb's words). A few comments follow:

1. I think Cobb is right about this shift from form to spirit, but with one caveat: I think that the shift only applies to what I refer to as 'official haiku'. Cobb was a founder of the British Haiku Society (BHS) and his interaction with ELH operated within the confines of that organization. The BHS holds roughly the same position in Britain that the Haiku Society of America (HSA) has in the U.S. Both of them are concerned with acting as gatekeepers and definers of what constitutes ELH.

As I have said elsewhere, these official societies, along with their journals, resemble gated communities. What is happening with ELH outside of their gated communities is, for the most part, unknown to them, and they are uninterested in finding out. My observation is that, outside of official ELH societies, the discussions about what constitutes haiku are still firmly centered on form.

2. Notice the split between form and spirit. It's not clear to me that seeing things in this dichotomous way makes sense. It does makes sense that free-verse ELH poets would want to shift discussions about ELH from form to something else because free-verse haiku has, by definition, rejected formal parameters; but it isn't clear why that something else would be 'spirit'.

3. The shift from form to spirit is, I think, a shift from objective criteria to subjective feeling. When free-verse ELH poets argue that there is a spirit to ELH (or haiku in general), and that they have access to it, they are privileging their subjectivity over objective, observable markers, such as the 5-7-5 form and season words.

4. I think it is possible to overcome this dichotomy. I would do so

by referring to the spirit of craft. A craft is the creative reshaping of material to specific standards and functions. A carpenter will reshape wood to make a table. A potter will reshape clay to make a cup. A knitter will reshape, or reconfigure, yarn to make a shawl. A gardener will reshape plants (think bonsai) into pleasing forms and arrangements. A musician reshapes the world of sound into melodies, harmonies and rhythms. The spirit of craft is to do this reshaping in the service of others; to create something that is both useful and attractive, something that makes life a little easier and contributes to the flourishing of our days. From this perspective, formal haiku is like shaping clay for a cup; or a carpenter taking wood and creating a table; or a knitter knitting a shawl to give to a friend. From this perspective, spirit and form merge.

5. I once saw someone post a poorly written poem in the 5-7-5 form on an online forum, and then ask the participants—particularly those adhering to 5-7-5—"Is that a haiku?" I don't remember the haiku that was posted, but it was something like:

> I like sandwiches,
> Peanut butter and jelly
> Is my favorite.

I responded that *yes*, it is a haiku. Why not? I added that I don't think it is a very good haiku, but a haiku nonetheless. I compared the haiku to an advertising jingle; I would call the jingle a song, but not a very good one. In fact, the jingle might be annoying. Still, it's a song.

Not all music is exalted, or even entertaining. And not all haiku are exalted, or even entertaining. Music has many functions, and so does haiku.

But if you start from the idea that

there is a special spirit, known to a special few through their intuition, then a poem like this would not be a haiku because it is not exalted. The problem is, how do we know when a poem has this exalted spirit? I have met ELH poets who have said that only a few of Basho's haiku are 'real' haiku; meaning, I think, that only a few of Basho's efforts have the spirit of haiku that they are looking for. Well, okay, but what if I think a haiku is just the best, and you don't? How do we proceed?

The formal advantage is that there are objective markers for deciding if it is a haiku. This is identical to examining a poem to decide if it is a sonnet or not (considering the number of lines, the rhyme scheme, metrics, etc.). This means that we share a common ground for beginning our conversation about the poem and whether or not it is a haiku. In contrast, there is no common ground if you start from your own subjectivity.

6. I blame Aristotle for a lot of this confusion. Aristotle critiqued a philosophical poem by Empedocles, complaining that it isn't really *poetry*, but mere *verse*. Homer, in contrast, was a real poet. Ever since then, western poets have been seeking to cast off the mere versifiers from the exalted realm of poetry, and have generated much confusion in the process.

7. A child might make a clumsy clay cup; but we'll put it in the kiln anyway because we appreciate the effort. Our first attempts at haiku might be clumsy as well, but they can be built upon, honed, and refined over the years. That is one of the secrets of a *craft* approach to spirit, of a *craft* approach to haiku. A craft approach is a path that has many way stations where new insights are gathered, or old insights refined.

8. I think sometimes these discussions and disagreements rest on a mistake involving category. The question as to whether or not a poem is a haiku differs from whether or not it is a good haiku. Using a formal approach, it is possible, in most instances, to answer the first question. From there, we can go on to discuss the second question. Using a subjective approach, it is often not possible to even answer the first question.

9. The fracturing of free-verse haiku into ever more approaches (monoku, visual-ku, incoherent-ku, four-line-ku, kitchy-kitchy-ku, etc.) is, I think, an inevitable result of this shift from form to subjective 'spirit'.

10. A formal approach to haiku can be taught. The steps are simple. First step, count syllables on your fingers. Second step, shape words into lines of 5-7-5 syllables. Third step, include a reference to season, nature or time. After that it becomes more complicated: there are a lot of possibilities for the fourth step. But I'm not sure how to go about teaching something like a 'haiku spirit'.

11. Clark Strand likes to say that there are haiku that overflow with meaning. The metaphor I use for this overflowing is striking a bell. Reading a haiku like this is like striking a bell: the sound of the bell continues, reverberating in the heart and mind. A bell has a form. The form of the bell is what makes it sonorous.

12. If I were to unpack the spiritual dimension of haiku, I think I would turn to our haiku ancestors and how they are present, and how they guide us, and speak to us across the centuries. There is something remarkable about this, a sense of communication that is difficult to define, but which is definitely there, kindly guiding us into the future.

Haiku

A bicycle ride   seven roaring lawnmowers   along the long way

— Priscilla Lignori

cicada chorus
their prophecy of autumn
cannot be ignored

— Sari Grandstaff

these evening shadows
wood duck sings himself to sleep –
autumn at the pond

— Michael Lustbader

dandelion tea
grandmother's bedtime stories
steeping in memory

her ceramic bowl
was kept in the guest bedroom –
one day it was gone

— Neil Whitman

Hippo shape in stone
stands vigil until low tide
when its calves come home

— Danielle Woerner

At the laguna
A heron stands on the shore –
Guardian of dreams.

— Jim Wilson

Raindrops in oceans
Magically watery
To swim or to float?

— Rose Menyon Heflin

The cicadas hide
from a rising bonfire
that touches the moon

Autumn moves slowly—
the wild stream through gilded pine—
there, I rest my thoughts

— Sher Ting

Forested hillside
So far off in the distance
Calls to me loudly

Predatory owl
Watching from a low tree branch
And missing nothing

— Rose Menyon Heflin

A flock of colors
Ride on the brisk autumn air
To kiss my shoulders

— Michael T. Smith

From fire-kissed skies,
a quiver of ochre light
rests in open palms

Autumn's harvest moon
ribs our lungs with filtered gold,
a breath of dewdrops

— Sher Ting

A gentle rustle
Wild geranium carpet
Follow the anger

— Rose Menyon Heflin

tapestries of leaves
drop into carpets weaving
on the forest floor

— William Dennis

Deflated football
weighing down a pile of leaves
in the windswept yard

— R. W. Watkins

half a hurricane
comes to strip tree branches bare
leaves a memory

days are shortening
swallows perch upon the wire
Africa awaits

— Steve Denehan

geese fly south over
river mist and chimney smoke
and turned-up faces

— William Dennis

melancholy songs
floating gray in autumn mist
loons circle and call

our pace slows amidst
leaves that are now edged with frost—
welcoming autumn

— Michael Lustbader

Moonlit sparkling frost –
On the shelf an empty space
For a book that's lost.

I take from the shelf
A book I never finished –
Talking to the dead.

— Jim Wilson

tarot reader's porch
waiting for my appointment
the wind chimes and me

— Sari Grandstaff

The name on the plaque
Is someone I do not know –
Brown grass that's cut back.

— Jim Wilson

With a paring knife,
I hollow Autumn's marrow
into pumpkin pie

— Sher Ting

A missing spider—
its splintered web left behind
inside the lampshade

— Priscilla Lignori

Grandchildren disguised
as a ladybug and bee—
a cell-phone photo

— James Lignori

People with face masks
Practicing the distance dance,
And autumn shadows.

— Jim Wilson

A murder of crows
The deepest of ebony
Is it an omen?

Roses, pretty and pink
Riddled with blood-thirsty thorns
Still abloom outside

— Rose Menyon Heflin

Born in September
it's still November's flower—
the chrysanthemum

— Priscilla Lignori

Resplendent pansy
flames red in strawberry jar
defies freezing breeze

Row of dried weeds
hissing in the wind defines
neighbors' boundaries

Arms of Russian sage
still stretch up toward the sky:
bones recall green life

— Danielle Woerner

Dim November light
The sword of the moon glowing
and the frightened stars.

— Jim Wilson

her unblinking eyes
the sky painted with fireworks
clouds hiding the moon

  — Steve Denehan

tonight candle flames
come together to make
this conflagration

smoothed by candlelight
the face she turns is someone
I had forgotten

wind snuffs a candle
but makes the fireplace roar—
happy fiftieth

  — William Dennis

curtains and doors closed
we hibernate together
and forget the sun

  — Steve Denehan

November's ending –
The silence of the wind-chimes
As the mute moon sets.

December morning,
The steadily falling rain,
So many voices.

  — Jim Wilson

noir streetlights in fog
the world trembles in puddles
lonely barking dog

  — Steve Denehan

Assessing the Fruits of the Moonlight Haiku Challenge

R. W. Watkins

It was announced in the late summer of this year that the Consulate-General of Japan in Toronto was inviting poets to submit haikus throughout September as part of their Moonlight Haiku Challenge. "...We will be accepting submissions of original haiku honouring the Harvest Moon," stated their official webpage, "this year on Oct. 1. At a time when life presents countless distractions, this is an opportunity to collectively breathe, admire the beauty of the moon, and enjoy the old Japanese custom of Tsukimi (autumn moon viewing)."

It was the organisers' original requirement that all submissions be written in the traditional 5-7-5 form; however, as reported in my forward to *Eastern Structures* No. 15, certain pathetic hacks at Haiku Canada soon complained, and subsequently sweet-talked the challenge's administrators into changing the rules to accommodate their sheer lack of poetic ability. An official update stated: "We are no longer requiring the traditional 5-7-5 syllable form. However, since haiku is conventionally considered to be the shortest poem in the world, three-line haiku are desirable."

One-hundred and fifty-two people contributed 201 poems (several of which took the form of photographic haiga) to the challenge, and the compiled results were published as a PDF anthology in early November. Copies were sent by email to contributors, which included Yours Truly. As one might expect, the results were mixed, ranging from the impressive to the generic to the downright feeble. Such results obviously reflected the 'requested' change in guidelines.

Appropriately enough, the anthology opens with a message and a haiku in Japanese from Mr. Sasayama Tukuya, the Consul-General of Japan in Toronto. "The Moonlight Haiku Challenge was one of the first projects I contributed to upon taking my post as Consul-General of Japan in Toronto," he writes. "We usually learn how to write a haiku at the school in Japan and thus I am submitting my own haiku for the first time in a while."

The Consul-General's introduction is followed ever so cordially, if not successfully, by a haiku apiece from three "honoured guests"; namely, the Honourable Elizabeth Dowdeswell, Lieutenant Governor of Ontario; Her Worship Bonnie Crombie, Mayor of Mississauga; and cookbook author Mary Berg, host of *Mary's Kitchen Crush* (I dare not google!) – all accompanied with photographs that feature varying degrees of smiling, of course. Of the three dubious inclusions, only Mayor Crombie's demonstrates any rudimentary knowledge of the haiku form:

Missing Kariya
Our friends under the same moon
Far across the sea

I'd like to think that "Kariya" refers to the city in Japan, or the park in Mississauga named for it; but given the Canadian context, I wouldn't be the least surprised if it were a reference to NHL Hall-of-Fame left-winger Paul Kariya, who officially retired from active playing in June of 2011.

It is the names more familiar in poetry circles whose submissions comprise the main body of the anthology. Not unexpectedly, those known for composing primarily in the traditional 5-7-5 form deliver the most satisfying and definitive haiku:

> that eye in the sky
> lidded with pieces of cloud…
> the sun or the moon?

> — Amy Losak

> Moon rises slowly
> over the golden wheat field
> The deer are entranced

> — Priscilla Lignori

I think it's also safe to say that such workers in the 5-7-5 form also provide the most original contributions; e.g.:

> just a while ago,
> that crescent-shaped nail clipping
> was a harvest moon

> — Becka Chester

Not surprisingly, the majority of these traditional haijins are from the United States; but there is the occasional Canadian who has the gumption and talent to work within more definite parameters—Canadians such as the Ontario-born editor of *The Asahi Shimbun*'s Asahi Haikuist Network column:

> alone in my home
> arranging the casket spray
> a red maple moon

> — David McMurray

From the free-form side of the haiku fence comes a more noticeably 'mixed bag'. Some poets certainly chose to take advantage of the change in guidelines, and used the challenge as a forum for the minimal and mundane; e.g.:

> parting ways—
> we each take
> the moon

> — Pamela Cooper

This is the sort of minimalist, thematically generic drivel that has increasingly littered the pages of the haiku societies' in-house journals over the past two decades or more. It's only reasonable that it should invade a venue like this one, with the guards let down.

Thankfully, it appears that some other poets known primarily for their free-verse approach to haiku made a conscious effort to conform to the specifics of the 5-7-5 form as best they could. Maybe they thought that there would be a bias in favour of the traditional structure regardless of the change in guidelines; maybe they submitted their haikus before the change was announced. Whatever the reasons, one can easily detect the struggles inherent in the attempts of Harvey Jenkins, Mark Bushell, Joanne Morcom and Claudia Coutu Radmore—names all recognisable from Haiku Canada publications. Others were more successful in their endeavours, both preserving the 5-7-5 dynamic and creating Zen-like moments of greater seeing:

> harvest moon viewing —
> the glow of mother's seashells
> on the windowsill

> — Roberta Beary

the shadowy moon
above my sad apartment
shines above you too

— Michael Dylan Welch

a sudden shiver
moon that turns the plums scarlet
turns my face to you

— Dorothy Mahoney

I should note that Hans Jongman, Anne-Marie Labelle and Lorraine A. Padden also managed to contribute respectable poems of the traditional persuasion. Gratefully, there were no contributions from *Haiku Canada Review* editor Mike Montreuil or evangelical hack Terry Ann Carter. This wasn't a complete no-talent show.

Sadly, there is a certain shoddiness apparent in the editing that plagues this little anthology, however. Omissions and typos are definitely apparent. For example, in the following, we are left to presume that the word 'eye' has been omitted from the end of the second line:

golden grasses dance
beneath the moon's watchful –
harvest guardian

— Lisa Mulrooney

The main body of English-language poems is followed by a six-page section of Japanese haiku. Unfamiliar with the language unfortunately, I cannot comment as to the structural specifics and success or failure of these verses.

The Japanese-language poems are followed by a quaint two-page section of English-language attempts by third- and fourth-grade pupils of Japanese from the Okanagan Waldorf School in Lumby, British Columbia. I'm not sure if the boys and girls in question will react positively when they rediscover this PDF file a decade or two from now, but I guess they can always blame their teacher and parents if poems such as the following bring them embarrassment:

The silver wolf trots
Along a path by a creek
He howls at the moon

— Zoe Freller (4th grade)

The children's poems are followed by a page of haiku from the Consulate-General's Toronto staff. Apparently no better qualified than the three 'honoured guests', the four staff members have chosen to remain anonymous, interestingly.

The anthology concludes with a note from the editor, who, oddly enough, is never officially identified either.

Although the odds were stacked against it, the *Moonlight Haiku Challenge Anthology* is far from a complete failure. This is due in no small part to the (mostly American) 5-7-5 haiku poets who answered the call, and the free-form haijins who dared to be traditional. More importantly, I think the project demonstrates the potential of such haiku challenges in the future. The anonymous editor, I should note, insists that the Consulate-General's staff shall begin discussions to plan another such challenge. So I would advise worthy haiku poets to check in with the Consulate-General's website from time to time, and to flood the staff with their best 5-7-5 haiku, given the opportunity. You have nothing to lose except your apathy and self-doubt.

Senryu (or Haiku in a Lighter Vein)

Rose-filled barrios
Their streets chattering with dance
Love amid garbage

Never imagined
Amish eating McDonald's
Train station surprise

— Rose Menyon Heflin

sea gulls are asking
Where did all the people go?
no fries to pick up

one word out of two –
place and personality
define the skylark

sleep impossible –
voices of the bell crickets
then my alarm rings

— Neil Whitman

The T.V.'s too loud
And it's a Spanish station—
But the food is good.

— Jim Wilson

Covid Halloween
pumpkin spice and all things nice
horror all around

— Steve Denehan

homemade raisin wine
father's secret recipe
is a secret, still

my instructor blind
but his hands somehow had eyes –
my first flute lesson

— Neil Whitman

All my structured clothes
donned for concerts, office, guests
traded for PJs

— Danielle Woerner

first wind in the pines
two large limbs land on our roof –
a budget-buster

a bank for acorns
the yield on my deposit
grows at sky-high rates

— Neil Whitman

Anorexia –
The haiku poet deletes
One more syllable.

— Jim Wilson

A mental tattoo
Both imaginary and
Unforgettable

— Rose Menyon Heflin

winter on the way
this is not a metaphor
though it feels like one

unlit corkscrew curls
summer gone, not yet winter
we live in between

— Steve Denehan

Mike Alexander was born in 1959 in New York City. He has worked in bookstores, banks, liquor stores and corporate offices. He passed through a few New Jersey rock bands in the 1980s. Since 1990, he has produced a number of chapbooks, the most recent of which was *We Internet in Different Voices* (Modern Metrics). His poems have appeared in numerous print journals, from the likes of *Abridged, Atlanta Review, Borderlands, Circumference, Contemporary Ghazals*, *Heavenbone* and *Iota*, to *Link, Measure, Newark Review, Other Poetry, Raintown Review, River Styx* and *Texas Review*. Online, he has participated in such sites as *Barefoot Muse, Capriole, Chimera, Folly, MiPoesias, Now Culture, Scheherazade's Behest, Shit Creek Review*, and *Worm*. For more than ten years, he administrated The Sonnet Board, an on-line poetry workshop dedicated to the sonnet. Alexander has presided over hundreds of readings, from Paterson, New Jersey to Houston, Texas. He lives with his wife, the poet, K. A. Thomas.

Steve Denehan lives in Kildare, Ireland with his wife Eimear and daughter Robin. He is the author of two chapbooks and one collection with several collections forthcoming, including *Days of Falling Flesh and Rising Moons* from Golden Antelope Press, due for publication in October of 2020. Twice winner of the *Irish Times*'s New Irish Writing prize, his numerous publication credits include *Poetry Ireland Review, Acumen, Westerly* and *Into The Void*. He has been nominated for Best of the Net, Best New Poet, and has been twice nominated for The Pushcart Prize.

William Dennis spent two years in Peace Corps Nepal, marrying on his return to the US, his present wife, Nancy, who had lived three years in central India. Together, they adopted five children from India. The foundation for interest in the popular ghazal form was sparked to life while passing through Delhi to take part in their eldest daughter's wedding. Although he has written in a great many forms of verse and prose, he has been returning to the ghazal for twenty years. He lives in the jungles of Pennsylvania.

Laura Z. Fairgrieve received her MFA from Adelphi University. She is a recipient of the 2016 Poets & Writers Amy Award. Her poems appear in the anthology *Women of Resistance: Poems for a New Feminism* published by O/R Books. Her work has appeared in *Arkana, Inscape, Mortar* Magazine, *Underwater New York, Ink in Thirds*, and *The Bitchin' Kitsch*, among others. She lives in Brooklyn.

Sari Grandstaff is a high-school librarian. Her work has appeared in *TheNewVerse.News* and other print and online journals. In March of 2018 she had one of her haiku displayed just a few short blocks from the White House. She is a member of the Haiku Society of America and the Hudson Valley Haiku-Kai. She is also the founder of National Haiku Poetry Day, which has since come under the auspices of The Haiku Foundation. She resides in Woodstock, New York, with her husband and three children.

S. Haina was born in Wales to Pakistani parents. She aims to energize her writing by focusing on imagery and fluidity. She is a fan of traditional forms such as ghazal and haiku. This is Haina's first published ghazal. One can read more of her poems on Instagram (@s.haina.writes).

Aafaq Hameed was born in the Kashmiri town of Bijbehara. A young poet, his work demonstrates the skill and knowledge of a bard beyond his years, and has been published in various magazines and posted on poetry blogs.

Rose Menyon Heflin is an emerging poet and artist from Wisconsin. So far, her work has appeared in *Argot Magazine, the Aurorean, Haiku Journal, Haikuniverse, One Sentence Poems*, and the Wisconsin Fellowship of Poets' Calendar. She also has work forthcoming in *Bramble* and *Three Line Poetry*.

Mace Hosseini is a retired professional engineer whose avocations include painting and writing poetry. His e-book of poems and paintings, *The Lessons of the Soul*, is available from Amazon.com. He resides in LaSalle, Ontario, Canada.

James Lignori taught high-school English for 34 years, and is the recipient of the N.Y. State's English Council's Excellence in Teaching award. A life-long spiritual seeker, he has studied many traditions, and has been a student of Richard Rohr, Clark Strand and other spiritual teachers. In the last twenty years, he has facilitated many spiritual groups. He currently offers Spiritual Companioning to individuals and groups. He is an active member of Hudson Valley Haiku-kai, a group of poets that meet to share and discuss their haiku poems.

Priscilla Lignori is the winner of numerous international awards for haiku poetry, including the 2013 Basho Award and the 2016 Kiyoshi and Kiyoko Tokutomi Memorial Haiku Contest. The founder and teacher of Hudson Valley Haiku-kai, a haiku group that meets once a month, she has published one book of haiku poetry, *Beak Open, Feet Relaxed: 108 Haiku.* She is a psychotherapist in private practice in New York State.

Michael Lustbader studied at Columbia University in NYC, as well as Adephi University in Garden City, New York. An accomplished photographer as well as a poet, he resides in Lakeway, Texas.

Michael T. Smith is an Assistant Professor of English who teaches both writing and film courses. He has published over 150 pieces (poetry and prose) in over eighty different journals. He loves to travel.

John W. Steele is a psychologist, yoga teacher, assistant editor of *Think: A Journal of Poetry, Fiction and Essays*, and graduate of the MFA Poetry Program at Western Colorado University. His poetry has appeared or is forthcoming in *Amethyst Review, Boulder Weekly, Buddhist Poetry Review, Blue Unicorn, Colorado Sun, Copperfield Review, The Lyric, Mountains Talking, New Verse News, The Orchards, Peacock Journal*, and *Verse-Virtual*. He won *The Lyric*'s 2017 Fall Quarterly Award, won an award in the 2020 Soul-Making Keats Literary Competition, and was awarded Special Recognition in the 2019 Helen Schaible International Sonnet Contest. His book reviews have appeared in *Cha: An Asian Literary Journal*, and *Raintown Review*. Steele lives in Boulder, Colorado and enjoys hiking in the mountains.

Alison Stone has published six full-length collections: *Caught in the Myth* (2019), *Dazzle* (2017), *Masterplan* (a book of collaborative poems with Eric Greinke, 2018), *Ordinary Magic* (2016), *Dangerous Enough* (2014), and *They Sing at Midnight*, which won the 2003 Many Mountains Moving Poetry Award; as well as three chapbooks. Her poems have appeared in *The Paris Review, Poetry, Ploughshares, Barrow Street, Poet Lore*, and many other journals and anthologies. She has been awarded *Poetry*'s Frederick Bock Prize and the *New York Quarterly*'s Madeline Sadin Award. She was the 2017 recipient of LitSpace St. Petersburg Writer's Residency. She is also a painter and the creator of The Stone Tarot. A licensed psychotherapist, she has private practices in NYC and Nyack.

Sher Ting lived in a land of eternal summer, otherwise known as Singapore, for nineteen years, before spending the next five years in medical school in Australia. She has been published in *Trouvaille Review* and *Eunoia Review*, among others. She is currently an editor of a creative arts-sharing space, known as INLY Arts.

R. W. Watkins created and published *Contemporary Ghazals*, the world's first English-language journal dedicated to the ghazal form. He is the only Canadian included in Agha Shahid Ali's *Ravishing DisUnities*, the world's first anthology of English-language ghazals. In the 1990s and 2000s, Watkins's haiku and related verse appeared most prominently in *Lynx*, *RAW NerVZ Haiku* and Haiku Canada publications. He also published three chapbooks of said poetry. Online, he edits *The Comics Decoder* journal, and has served as an assistant poetry editor at *Red Fez*. His major works include *Trinity*, which collects his aforementioned chapbooks with bonus material; *Direct Lines To Hell*, a collection of his early free verse; and *The Rites of Summer*, an experimental novella set amidst the youthful decadence of Eastern Canada in 1980. *Waka-Cola: A Tanka Guide to Pop Art* and *small flowers crack concrete: eyeku and conceptual minimalism* are his latest chapbooks.

Neal Whitman resides in Pacific Grove, California, with his wife, Elaine, where they retired as professional educators. Both are award-winning members of the Yuki Teikei Haiku Society. Neal is Vice President of the United Haiku and Tanka Society and haiku editor for *Pulse: Voices from the Heart of Medicine*. In 2019, Neal's haiku won Best US in the Vancouver Cherry Blossom Festival and Gold Medical in the Ito En North American Grand Prix. Neal is the author of a haiku collection, *From this Moment On*, and a tanka collection, *How Pleasant It Is*, published by Cyberwit (2020).

Jim Wilson has led a life that has many twists and turns. He worked on the trans-Alaska pipeline, studied in Korea and Japan, and is a former Buddhist monk and prison chaplain. He currently runs a spiritual book and tea shop in northern California. He is also a member of a local Quaker group. A dozen books of poetry to his credit, Wilson has a strong interest in syllabic forms, which is the focus of his *Shaping Words* blog. In yet another existence, Wilson was better known as Tundra Wind, the creator and publisher of *APA-Renga*—or *Lynx*, as incoming editor Terri Lee Grell renamed it—the world's first English-language journal dedicated to the Japanese linked-verse form.

Michael Wilson, a writer living in Lexington, Kentucky, has had work published in several small journals, including *Appalachian Heritage*, *Solidago*, *Frogpond*, *Cagibi*, *Stoneboat* and *The Aurorean*.

Danielle Woerner is a singer, writer and teacher who lives on the Downeast Maine coast, where she is co-founder and President of the Sunrise County Arts Institute. Her haiku have been published in the Hudson Valley arts/culture monthly *Chronogram* and the *Three Nations Anthology: Native, Canadian & New England Writers* (Resolute Bear Press, 2017). Her features and op-ed pieces have appeared in *Classical Singer*, *New Music Connoisseur*, *Hudson Valley* magazine and *Newsweek*. Her reporting for weekly newspapers was acknowledged in 2018 by the National Federation of Press Women. Woerner, also a BMI-affiliated songwriter, began writing haiku in earnest ten years ago—initially to recover from generating a 50,000-word NaNoWriMo novel manuscript in thirty days—and joined the Hudson Valley Haiku-kai in 2013.

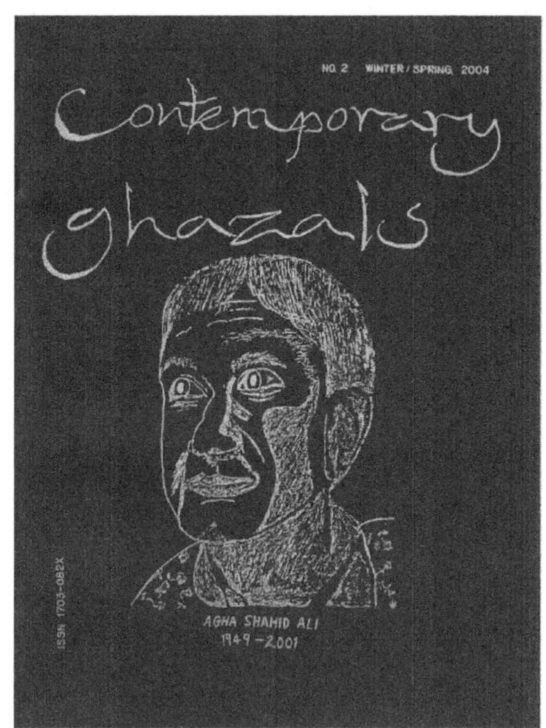

Copies of *Contemporary Ghazals* Nos. 1 and 2 are still available for $4 ppd. each. Please send postal money order or well-concealed cash to P.O. Box 111, Moreton's Harbour, NL, A0G 3H0, Canada. For more information or assistance, please get in touch at nocturnaliris@gmail.com.

Also from *Nocturnal Iris*:

The Complete Eastern Structures / Volume Two — Issues 6 through 10 in one handy omnibus!
Wholly Trinities — The Nocturnal Iris Anthology of Sijo in English!
Available in paperback at Amazon.com